FLYING INTO CHRISTMAS

Pop and Fiddle duets for two Violas

Book One

arr. Myanna Harvey

Cover Painting:
Moonbike, Greg Harvey (acrylic on canvas)

CHP440

©2022 by C. Harvey Publications® All Rights Reserved.

www.charveypublications.com - print books & free sheet music blog
www.learnstrings.com - downloadable books & chamber music

FLYING INTO CHRISTMAS

POP AND FIDDLE DUETS FOR TWO VIOLAS, BOOK ONE

all duets arranged by Myanna Harvey

Table of Contents

*Used by permission, listed on each duet page.

Flying Into Christmas for Two Violas, Book One

Jingle Bell Rock

arr. M. Harvey

JINGLE BELL ROCK
Words and Music by JOE BEAL and JIM BOOTHE
Copyright © 1957 (Renewed) CHAPPELL & CO., INC.
This Arrangement © 2022 CHAPPELL & CO., INC.
All Rights Reserved Used by Permission of ALFRED MUSIC
Sole Selling Agent of this 2022 arrangement: C. Harvey Publications®
It is illegal to photocopy or reproduce the music in this book.

Reel on the Housetop

Hanby, arr. M. Harvey

Winter Wonderland

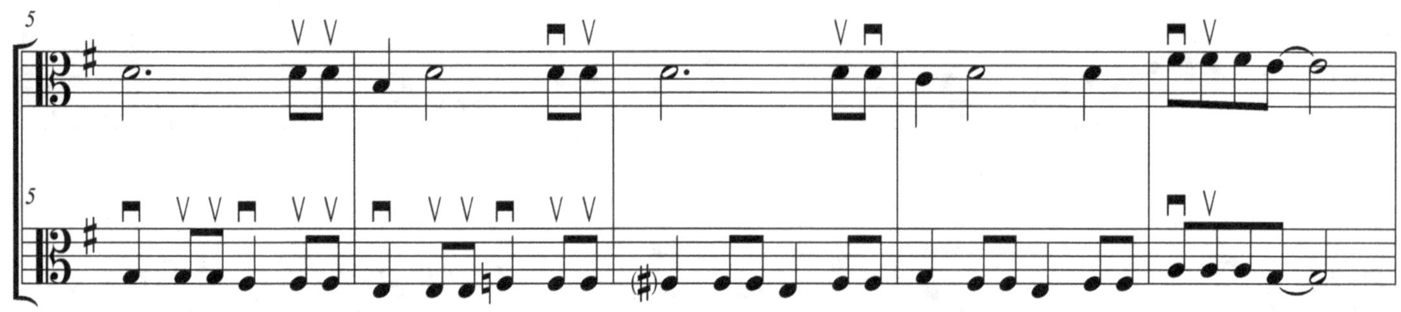

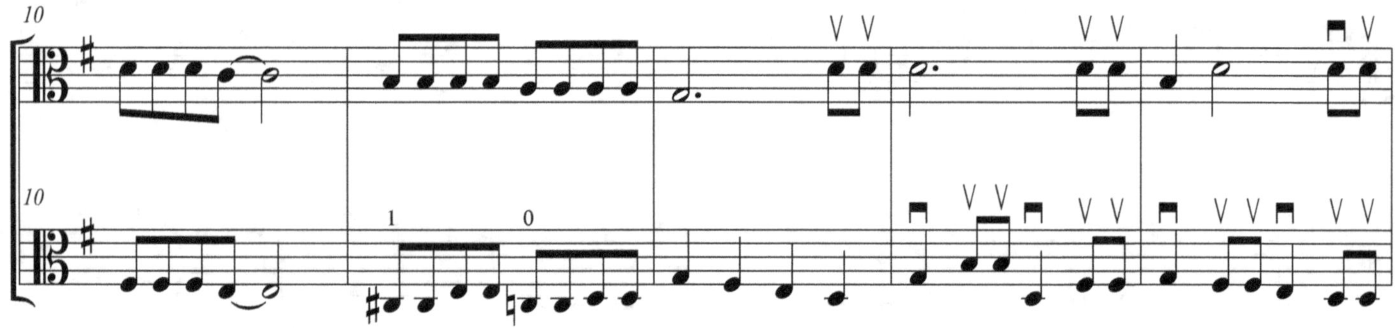

Jingle Bell Jig

Pierpont, arr. M. Harvey

Fine
D.S. al Fine

The Little Drummer Boy

arr. M. Harvey

THE LITTLE DRUMMER BOY
Words and Music by KATHERINE DAVIS, HENRY ONORATI and HARRY SIMEONE
Copyright © 1958 (Renewed) EMI MILLS MUSIC, INC. and INTERNATIONAL KORWIN CORP.
Exclusive Worldwide Print Rights Administered by ALFRED MUSIC
This Arrangement © 2022 EMI MILLS MUSIC, INC. and INTERNATIONAL KORWIN CORP.
All Rights Reserved Used by Permission of ALFRED MUSIC
Sole Selling Agent of this 2022 arrangement: C. Harvey Publications®

We Wish You a Hoedown Christmas

Trad., arr. M. Harvey

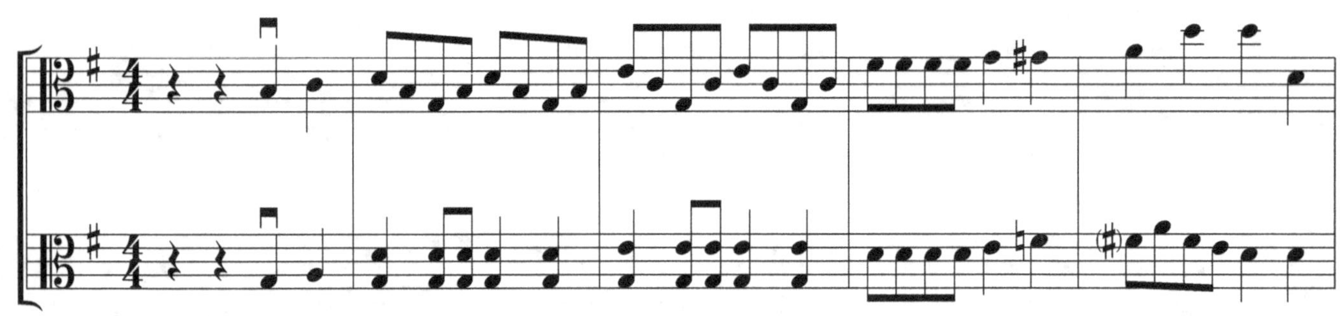

Frosty the Snowman

arr. M. Harvey

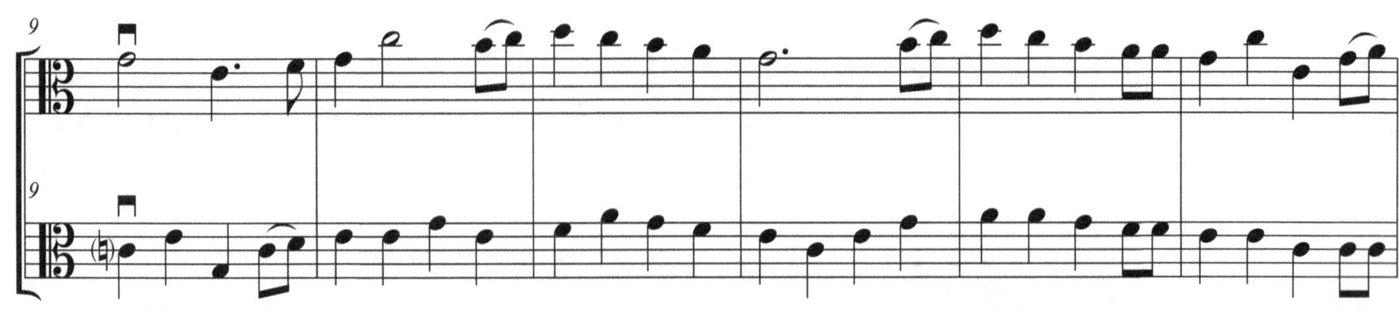

Bell Carol Dance

Leontovych, arr. M. Harvey

Have Yourself a Merry Little Christmas

arr. M. Harvey

HAVE YOURSELF A MERRY LITTLE CHRISTMAS
Words and Music by HUGH MARTIN and RALPH BLANE
Copyright © 1943 (Renewed) METRO-GOLDWYN-MAYER INC.
© 1944 (Renewed) EMI FEIST CATALOG INC.
All Rights (Excluding Print) Controlled and Administered by EMI FEIST CATALOG INC.
Exclusive Worldwide Print Rights Controlled and Administered by ALFRED MUSIC
This Arrangement © 2022 EMI FEIST CATALOG INC. All Rights Reserved Used by Permission of ALFRED MUSIC
Sole Selling Agent of this 2022 arrangement: C. Harvey Publications®

Rock the Halls

Trad., arr. M. Harvey

Let it Snow! Let it Snow! Let it Snow!

arr. M. Harvey

Dance of the Three Kings

Hopkins, arr. M. Harvey

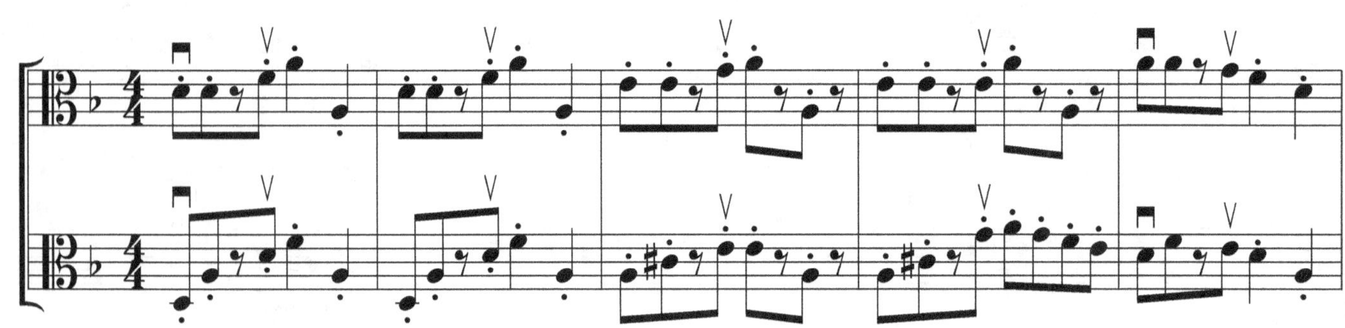

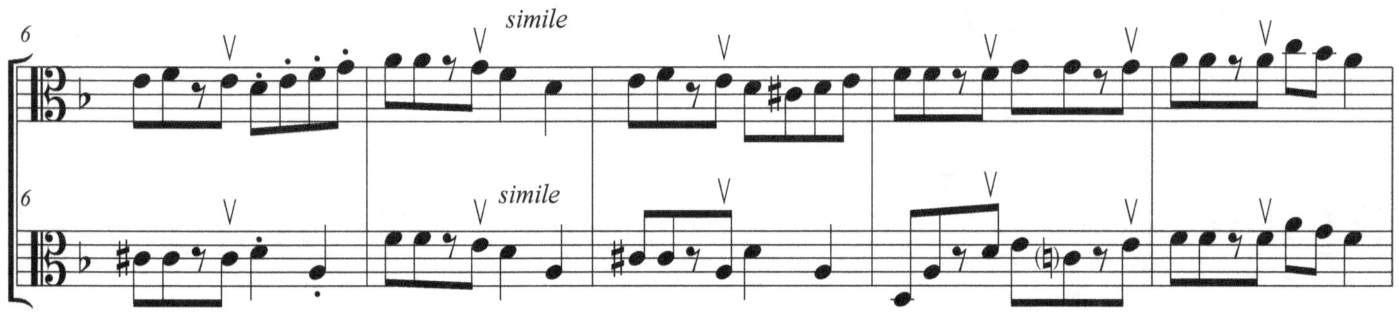

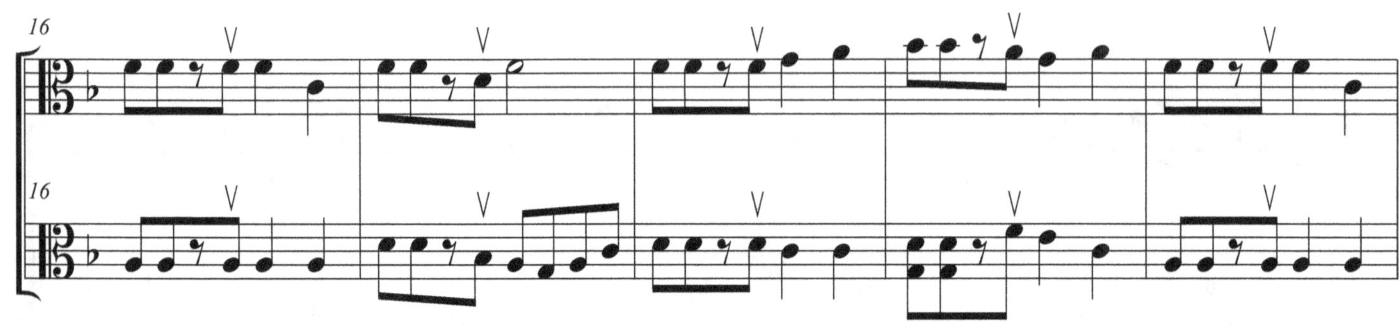

Parade of the Tin Soldiers

Jessel, arr. M. Harvey

The Goose is Getting Fat

Trad., arr. M. Harvey

Dance of the Reed Flutes from *The Nutcracker*

Tchaikovsky, arr. M. Harvey

Toyland from *Babes in Toyland*

Herbert, arr. M. Harvey

March of the Toys from *Babes in Toyland*

Herbert, arr. M. Harvey

You Might Also Like:

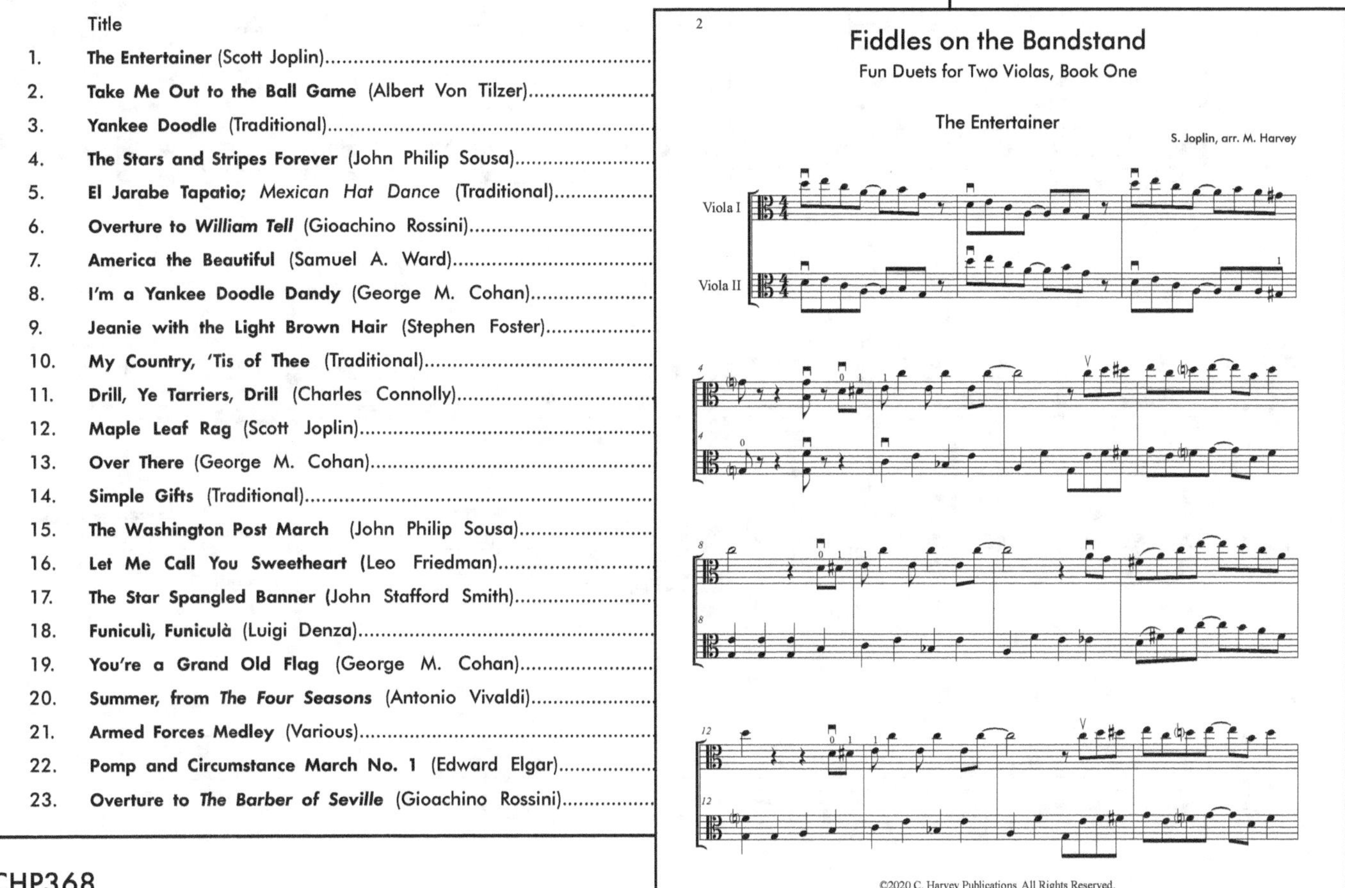

Fiddles on the Bandstand: Fun Duets for Two Violas
Book One

all duets arranged by Myanna Harvey

Table of Contents

CHP368
www.charveypublications.com

Take a journey to a simpler time when lawn chairs and blankets would be out under the stars and music would waft out from under the eaves of the wooden bandstand.

These are the tunes that got our feet moving, made us smile, and brought us together. Now, with these viola duets, you can bring the toe-tapping, exuberant joy to others and remind us all that through highs and lows, music can be something we share to keep our spirits up and build community.

From Scott Joplin to John Philip Sousa, these viola duets will invite you up on the bandstand, out for a gig, or out on your lawn to play your heart out! Know any violinists or cellists? You can pick up a copy of the violin or cello book and play with those instruments as well; the viola book is fully compatible with the violin and cello books.

This viola book is in first and third positions and is at an intermediate level.

Flying Fiddle Duets for Two Violas, Book One

John Ryan's Polka

Trad., arr. Myanna Harvey

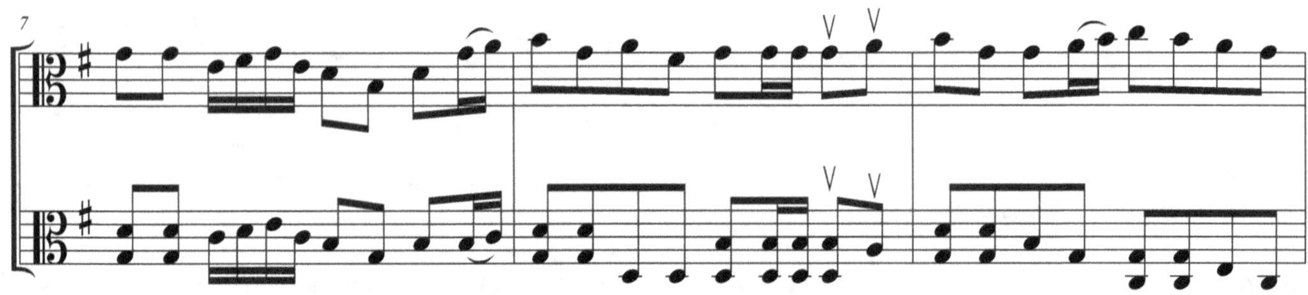